GET OVER THESE, TOO!

*More Truth About
What You Know
That Just Ain't So!*

Paul Hasselbeck, DDS
Bil Holton, Ph.D.

This publication is designed to provide accurate and authoritative information in regard to the subject matter covered. It is sold with the understanding that the publisher is not engaged in rendering legal, accounting or other professional service. *(From a Declaration of Principles jointly adopted by a Committee of the American Bar Association and a Committee of Publishers.)*

Publisher's Cataloging-in-Publication Data

Hasselbeck, Paul
Get Over These, Too! : More truth about what you know that just ain't so / Paul Hasselbeck and Bil Holton
    p. cm.

    ISBN 978-1-893095-56-4
Library of Congress Control Number: 2009926498

10   9   8   7   6   5   4   3   2   1

Dedicated to those brave Truth students who are ready to stretch their awareness even more — and move to a whole new level of understanding as they walk the spiritual path on practical feet!

Table of Contents

Introduction 1

Let Go, Let God 6

Nothing Good Ever Lasts 12

It Just Wasn't Meant to Be 18

God Has a Sense of Humor 24

This Is a Wake Up Call 30

It's In God's Hands 36

This Is What I Was Called To Do 42

The Universe Rushes In to Fill the Void . .48

What Goes Around Comes Around 54

When the Student is Ready,
   the Teacher Will Appear 60

This was Sent to Test Me 66

It Was An Act of God 72

That Person Pushes My Buttons 78

Everything Happens For a Reason 84

This or Something Better 90

Count It All Joy 96

Surrender It To God 102

Not My Will But God's Will Be Done . .108

I Behold the Christ in You 116

Whatever Will Be, Will Be 122

God Will Provide 128

This Must Be a Sign From God 134

God is Good All the Time 140

I'll Get There When I'm Ready 146

It's a God Thing 152

Summary Chart 158

Who Are these Authors? 161

Index 163

Introduction

Are you ready to be challenged again? Are you ready to question some of the euphemisms, platitudes and stock phrases you have been using in your everyday conversations? Are you ready to have more of your assumptions exposed and your comfort zone stretched? If so, this book is for you!

When we collected the phrases we debunked in *Get Over It!*, we thought we had pretty much exhausted the supply. However, we began to see and hear more and more of them wherever we went. This is what happens when we focus on something in consciousness. For example, when we decide to buy a particular car, we begin seeing that car everywhere.

We wrote *Get Over It!* because we were shocked that so many of those phrases were actually being used without questioning their meanings. We wrote *Get Over It!* hoping readers would have what we call "Duh-Ha" moments. A "Duh-Ha" moment is much like an "Ah-Ha" moment, except a "Duh-Ha" moment is when something that is obvious becomes, well, obvious! "Duh-Ha!"

Here we are once again, dishing up another helping of familiar euphemisms, platitudes, and stock phrases used by people who come from Unity, New Thought, and New Age backgrounds. Some we even hear from the general public. These phrases, like the ones in *Get Over It!*, are frequently part of the fabric of our everyday language. While each may contain a truth kernel, on closer inspection they do not accurately reflect Unity nor New Thought theology — or common sense, for that matter.

You may be asking yourself, why bother to get so picky about commonly used expressions? We're glad you asked! We believe many of these phrases are the result of embedded theological beliefs and attitudes we formed when we were younger. Using these warped phrases reinforces those beliefs and attitudes we thought we had outgrown when we left traditional faith customs. We unapologetically believe that when we try to get traction with one foot in Unity and New Thought theology while planting the other foot firmly in the concrete of the stale belief systems of our childhood, we keep ourselves stuck in the churchiness of embedded theology.

These phrases keep us glued to the old like a piece of bubble gum stuck to the bottom of our sneakers! This attachment to religiosity seriously threatens our ability to expand our consciousness and become more spiritually aware.

As we said in the introduction to the previous book, "We believe that if you want to dramatically enhance your spiritual walk, you'll consider the wisdom of the old saying attributed to Artemus Ward: 'It ain't the things we don't know that hurt us. It's the things we do know that ain't so!' Think about it. It's not so much the unanswered questions which keep us in the dark; it's the unquestioned answers (traditional, dogmatic beliefs) which keep us stuck in convention."

We believe that as you breeze through this group of sayings, you will be challenged to examine your current beliefs. We affirm that you will use this as an opportunity to claim something new, and grow into a greater awareness of not only your innate Divinity, but of your ability to master your human experience.

The beliefs that you and your ancestors have held in mind have become thought currents so strong that their course in you can be changed only by your resolute decision to entertain them no longer. They will not be turned out unless the ego through whose domain they run decides positively to adopt means of casting them out of his consciousness, and at the same time erects gates that will prevent their inflow from external sources.

(Charles Fillmore, The Twelve Powers of Man, Pg. 154)

So . . .
WHAT
ELSE DO
WE NEED
TO GET
OVER?

What This Phrase Assumes

This familiar phrase asks us to let God 'out there' handle some problematic situation for us. It is all about the Biblical God from our childhood who is the great 'fix-it-man' in the sky. It perpetuates the belief in a separate God (Universe) which knows better than we do what kind of good we should have.

GET OVER IT!

● ●

If there ever were a more misused and abused New Thought phrase, this would top our list. Hello! (We say that when we want to get your attention.) There is no external, puppeteer-like God in the sky handling everything in our lives. We're going to add a little more amperage to that last statement. Let go of a God 'out there' and embrace your own Godness. And let go of the embedded theology that has gotten you so intent on denying your own innate Divinity.

LET GO; LET GOD

9

Truth Triage

There is only One Power and One Presence: God (Divine Mind). "We" are NOT separate from that One Mind, One Presence. There is no need to give up or abdicate our power. But, there IS something we do need to release. That something is our sense-addicted personality/ego. And, we must let Oneness, Christ, shine forth. We must let Oneness, Christ, be in control.

In a sense, we must pry our fearful egos out of our lives and circumstances, and pray our Oneness into the forefront of our conscious awareness. Our Christ Individuality, our True Nature, must guide our human personality instead of our personality thinking it rules our consciousness.

REPLACEMENT PHRASE

Leash Ego;
Unleash Godness

What This Phrase Assumes

This highly-charged negative phrase is used quite literally to bash our goodness. It is an abdication of our personal power and of our ability to enjoy goodness over time. It is generally used to justify something good being lost as a consequence of the 'ephemeral nature' of good things. Quite frankly, it is a negative affirmation which strongly implies that bad things last and good things don't because that is our lot in life. Bad endures and good demurs seems to be the sentiment.

GET OVER IT!

● ● ● ● ● ● ● ● ● ● ● ● ● ● ● ● ● ● ● ●

This phrase, Nothing Good Ever Lasts, springs from embedded theology raising its ugly head. It perpetuates the myth that we are inherently bad (sinners), and therefore, undeserving recipients of goodness. It has a demeaning undercurrent which attempts to negate our worthiness to acquire and KEEP good things.

Please understand, we are NOT advocating unnecessary material consumption and attachment to things. We are strongly suggesting that you GET OVER the belief that 'nothing good lasts.' No one is saddled with bad things nor is good limited. In the relative realm (the physical universe), the only 'thing' that endures is change.

NOTHING GOOD EVER LASTS

Truth Triage

What we call 'good' DOES have a life expectancy in the physical world (relative realm). What we label as 'bad' has a life expectancy, too! All physical things are perishable. But that doesn't mean 'good' things are more perishable than 'bad' things. The only enduring Essence is the One Mind, God, Absolute Good. In the Absolute realm (the world of Spirit), this Good is without opposite. In the relative realm (the physical universe), we have the capacity to express as much of "the good, the bad, and the ugly" as we desire and choose at our current level of consciousness.

One more thing! We'd like to clarify our position on the concept of goodness and its repression by organized religion: We believe in Original Goodness, not original sin. We unabashedly assert that we (that means all human beings) are not inherently bad or sinners and therefore relegated to more and more bad. Our Divine Essence is Godness and therefore Absolute Goodness.

REPLACEMENT
PHRASE

Absolute Good
Ever Lasts

NOTHING GOOD EVER LASTS

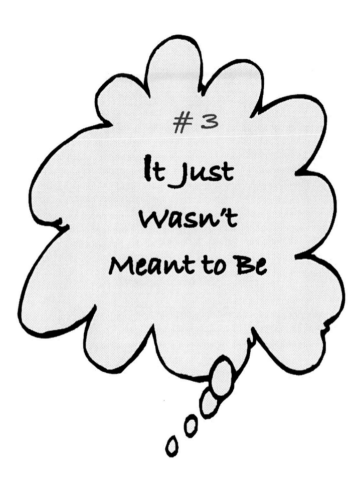

What This Phrase Assumes

This worn out phrase, (and similar ones such as "I'll get it if I was meant to have it" or "I guess I wasn't meant to have it") reinforces the idea that there is an external God (aka the "Universe") that determines what we can have, will have, or cannot have. We use these phrases when we want something and do not have it yet, or as a cop-out phrase to justify not getting something we want.

GET OVER IT!

● ●

There is no external God in the sky determining what we get or do not get. Nor is there a micromanaging deity who gives or withholds our good. The "Universe" is not a withholder of our good either. (The "Universe" is actually a New Age term that is really just another name for God, the God of our childhood).

The distorted belief that the Universe 'giveth this and taketh that' according to divine fiat is a belief we strongly encourage you to 'get over.' And by the way, there is also not a micromanaging deity who gives or withholds our good according to which side of the cloud it woke up on!

GET OVER THESE, TOO!

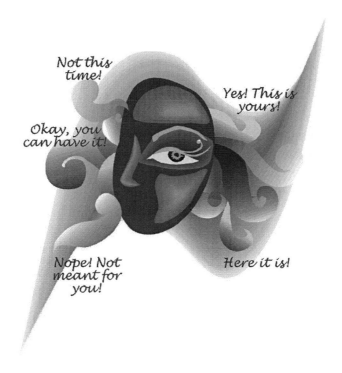

IT JUST WASN'T MEANT TO BE

Truth Triage

God, the One Mind, the Eternal Oneness is Principle which underwrites all of the Divine Ideas and Processes we use to create the experiences and the events of life. We are the ones who decide which of those processes we will employ to manifest our good. We determine what we have or don't have. We are the masters of our thoughts, words, and actions. If we mean to do something, and turn our intentions into actions, the chances of our accomplishing what we want move from possibility to probability to actuality.

REPLACEMENT
PHRASE

· ·

I'll Get It
If I Mean It

IT JUST WASN'T MEANT TO BE

What This Phrase Assumes

The phrase "God has a sense of humor" is used when something ironic or unexpected happens to us. The following, commonly used, expression captures the essence of this unfortunate phrase: "I laugh when God tells me His plan for my life. God laughs when I tell God my plan."

GET OVER IT!

● ●

We strongly encourage people who use this phrase – no, earnestly encourage them – no, adamantly encourage them – no, zealously encourage them to stop making God in their image! If that applies to you, please take our encouragement, earnestness, adamancy, and zealousness seriously. Stop making God in your image!

You're in good company, of course, if you insist on assigning human qualities to God – but because we have a keen sense of humor (you may have noticed) and a keener sense of purpose for writing this book, we invite you to 'get over' anthropomorphizing God.

GOD HAS A SENSE OF HUMOR

Truth Triage

God is not a gigantic person, white haired being, or white robed entity. God is Oneness, Absolute Good, Divine Mind, One Consciousness. God is Principle. Given that everything in the relative realm (the physical universe) is based on a Divine Idea, there must be some Divine Idea related to humor. However, this does not mean that God has a sense of humor or is humorous. Being humorous or having a sense of humor is what we do with Divine Ideas.

Here's our take on Divine humor-ology. Humor allows the Indwelling Spirit to enter through the rigid cracks in our consciousness. Humor ignites our laughter muscles. It acts like a sort of comedic acupuncture that smoothes out our rough edges. While a sense of humor does not apply to a God 'out there,' it is evidence of the Godness within us which expresses Itself as a Divinely ordered humorous thought. You may want to re-read that last sentence. Humor us. The next sentence can wait. Our sense is that if you got what we're suggesting, you'll allow Spirit to flow through the rigid cracks of your dogma so you can appreciate the metaphysics of humor. We propose that God is not humorous, but the essence of Humor Itself. We might say that if God is the Principle of Love, not loving; and God is the Principle of Life, not living; then God is the Principle of Humor, not funny or humorous.

REPLACEMENT
PHRASE

· ·

I Sense the Humor
in This

GOD HAS A SENSE OF HUMOR

What This Phrase Assumes

This saying is similar to the wooden phrase, "hit by a cosmic 2 x 4," which goes against the grain of some of the oldest and most revered of Truth Principles. We chipped away at it in our first Get Over It book. The phrase "wake up call" – like the phrase "hit by a cosmic 2x4" – is used when something troublesome happens to us. And the rationale is whatever happens is caused by God (the Universe) to wake us up. It implies that God 'out there' wants us to change in some way.

GET OVER IT!

· ·

There is no external God (aka the Universe, Entity, Divine Being, Divine Front Desk Clerk) who causes troublesome events to wake us up or get our attention. This tired phrase is another form of victim consciousness, the view that stuff happens to us because it is engineered by a meddling deity, or deities, who feel a compunction to keep us on the straight and narrow. While this phrase sounds like a sort of positive reprimand from 'on high,' it perpetuates a debilitating victim consciousness which, as we have chorused before, must be 'gotten over.'

THIS IS A WAKE UP CALL

Truth Triage

The truth is, while we might contribute to or even directly cause the events in our lives, they are not happening to wake us up. They happen because we "fall asleep" at the wheel of life! Then, in response to the untoward event, we decide whether we're going to wake up … or not. It's time to reiterate our 'get over it' sonnet: We must stay awake so we can take personal responsibility for our life experiences. How awake we stay depends on our *response-ability* as we handle our responsibilities.

Replacement Phrase

● ●

This is a
Wake Myself Up
Call!

What This Phrase Assumes

When something unpleasant or troublesome occurs, we may feel we do not know how to handle it. So, we throw up our hands and say, "It's in God's hands." The reasoning is somehow, someway, God (the Universe) will take care of everything.

GET OVER IT!

● ●

This phrase is based on the God of our childhood. It perpetuates the myth of a God in the sky. It abdicates our power to an external Deity. God is not a repairman or a handy man. This self-negating phrase endorses victim consciousness, because it is all about an anthropomorphic God (the Universe) acting to resolve our life problems.

IT'S IN GOD'S HANDS

Truth Triage

It's in our hands! It is our own Godness, our True Essence, from which we can deal with the troublesome circumstances we create from our human personalities/egos. We must claim our personal power over life's challenges. What we are is powerful beyond our imagination! "We" are Christ! (If you haven't wrapped your consciousness around that Truth yet, give yourself some more time. When you 'get' that you are Christ expressing at the point of you, at the point of your consciousness, you will find the inner peace, strength, confidence, and wisdom you need to live life to its fullest). Oh, and by the way, when we say we are Christ, we do not mean Jesus. We mean we are the Divine Idea that is made up of ideas.

We do not have to sit back and wait for some whimsical, capricious, white bearded God dressed in a white robe to fix unpleasant or troublesome life problems. Through our Godness, Divine Mindness, we can use Divine Ideas, Principles and Processes to resolve our problems and life situations.

REPLACEMENT
PHRASE

● ●

It's in My
'God Hands'

IT'S IN GOD'S HANDS

What This Phrase Assumes

When we find some life purpose that seems to fit who we think we are, we use this phrase to indicate that God has called us to this specific purpose. It is a phrase that choruses traditional religious beliefs. It implies that a Michelangelean God in the sky has a specific life purpose that is part of some grand plan for us, because we are one of the chosen ones. It is used in the sense that this is what we are meant to do.

Get Over It!

. . . .

We feel 'called' by our own sense of incredulousness to offer what we believe to be a sane response to an insane assumption. There is no one or no thing 'out there' calling us to do or be anything. If there is a life purpose or calling for anyone, it is simply for each of us to be the best Christ we can be. Jesus showed us how to express Christ (the Idea made up of Ideas).

Our calling comes from our own consciousness of Oneness, from the awareness of our indivisible Divine Mind. Our calling is an inside-out proposition. It is an interior flowering that shows we are in the flow of our blossoming Christ Nature.

THIS IS WHAT I WAS CALLED TO DO

Truth Triage

God is Oneness. God is Principle. God is not a Spiritual Entity or Being calling each of us to do or be anything in particular. Each of us determines how it is we express the Truth of What we are. We express the Truth of What we are using who we are (personality/ego) as the vehicle. The Truth of What we are is Christ or the Christ Nature (the Divine Idea that contains Ideas). Nothing more and nothing less. Each of us determines the form and shape we give to It in this relative realm. When we "feel a call" we "feel" we are doing or being something that is in alignment with our Christ Nature and our particular mix of talents and abilities.

REPLACEMENT
PHRASE

· ·

This is What I'm Calling
Myself To Do

THIS IS WHAT I WAS CALLED TO DO

What This Phrase Assumes

This phrase is based on the belief that the Universe abhors a vacuum or void and will fill it. According to this reasoning, the Universe will fill the void with anything: good, bad, or indifferent. The idea is that we'd better decide what we're going to put into the void or suffer the consequences! And the way this phrase is used, it is more like a fear statement – as in, "You better watch out because the Universe rushes in to fill the void." The implication is that the Universe will fill it with something bad.

GET OVER IT!

● ●

The Universe doesn't void on us!(We couldn't resist this!) It is not waiting to rush in and fill a vacuum or void. The Universe simply is. It doesn't try to be anything but Universe. If you asked, it would probably say it's perfectly happy being Universe.

And one more thought: how can there ever be a void if Divine Mind, Oneness, is everywhere present all the time? (We're just giving you something to think about!)

THE UNIVERSE RUSHES IN TO FILL THE VOID

Truth Triage

It is ironic that this phrase is an atypical 'Get Over It' phrase, in the sense that it implies we can take control and fill the void with something we really want **before** the Universe rushes in. The good news is we do not need to worry about the Universe filling a void with something. As we said, there really cannot be a void. The Truth is that when we rid our consciousness of a thought or belief we do not want, we need to focus on some new thought or belief we **do** want. Otherwise, we are likely to slip back to the old thinking

We are powerful creators and architects of our lives. Filling vacuums is in our spiritual DNA. We're going to ask you to put on your quantum physicist's hat for a moment, and share something about the Universe and YOU that is quite fascinating AND absolutely relevant to your spiritual – and human – growth and happiness. Are you interested? Okay. Here goes:

When half of a photon is "injected" into a quantum field (the field of infinite potential and possibility), a whole and complete photon emerges. What this might mean for us is that what we put into the quantum field of consciousness can be completed or brought into wholeness. Although we are not, and never can be, separate from the 'field,' we both act upon it and are the field at the same time.

Physicists call this quantum field of energy the Zero Point Field. This 'field' exists as energy with infinite potential that hasn't been formed into anything yet. However, from that infinite potential, literally anything can be formed. What physicists call the quantum field of energy is what philosophers and metaphysicians call consciousness.

REPLACEMENT PHRASE

• •

I Fill the Potential

#9

What Goes Around
Comes Around

54

What This Phrase Assumes

This phrase, like its sister phrase "what you send out comes back to you," is taken much too literally. Whatever we send out somehow, someway, sometime will come back seems to be the rationale. Send out anger, and anger will come back to us. If anger goes around, it generally generates more anger. Both of these phrases are normally used as warnings. They call for us to be careful for what we send out, because what we send out will come back to haunt us.

GET OVER IT!

● ●

These fear-veneered phrases perpetuate the myth that something 'out there' is keeping score of our activities and will see to it that we get what is coming to us if we misstep. What is sent out cannot come back because there is no 'back' to come to! There is only the present moment. If you have trouble wrapping your head around that last statement, take a few moments to let it come around again. (We're messing with you.) Seriously, though, the 'something' that seems as if it has come back is merely an event in consciousness that we assign relevance to, and make judgments about its value.

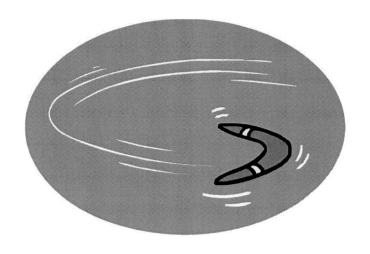

WHAT GOES AROUND COMES AROUND

Truth Triage

We do not experience the effects of what we send out or what goes around in the way commonly thought. Cause and effect are not separated in consciousness. You will probably want to read that last sentence again. If we "send out" anger, we do not have to wait for anger to 'come back around.' We experience the full force of the anger the moment we send it out (unleash it).

So, it makes sense to carefully consider what we send out. Not because it will come back sometime in the future, but because we experience its effects at the exact moment we create it.

REPLACEMENT
PHRASE

● ●

What We Send Out
is Already In

WHAT GOES AROUND COMES AROUND

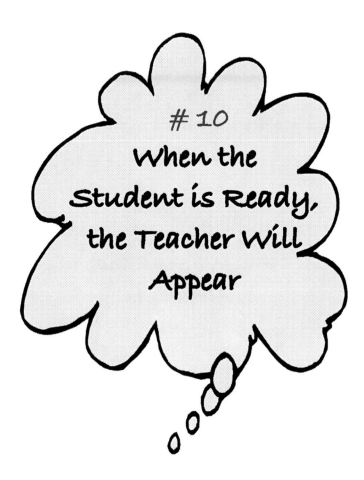

What This Phrase Assumes

There is a "gee wiz" factor when this phrase is used. It is used frequently to express amazement. Look everyone, this wonderful teacher appeared, as if by magic, just when I needed her or him! And surprise, it is the Universe (God) causing this teacher to appear.

GET OVER IT!

● ●

*God (the Universe) did not cause the teacher to appear. It is **us** who finally see what's already there! (Take your open palm and hit your forehead if you 'get' it').*

WHEN THE STUDENT IS READY, THE TEACHER
WILL APPEAR

Truth Triage

Each of us has a set of beliefs and attitudes. And, we see from and through these lenses. It is only when there is a shift in these beliefs and attitudes that we see the teacher who was there all along. Our readiness to see prepares us for the seeing. If we didn't have "the eyes to see," if we had not prepared ourselves, we would never have recognized the "teacher."

REPLACEMENT PHRASE

• •

When the Student
is Ready,
the Teacher
is Apparent.

What This Phrase Assumes

Once again we explore a phrase that retails an external something which seeks to correct our missteps. This something 'out there' mentality reinforces our supposed powerlessness and diminished capacity to determine the kind of life we want.

GET OVER IT!

●●●●●●●●●●●●●●●●●●●●●●

The following explanation may seem a bit testy, but that's what you've come to expect from us, right? We believe stretching your thinking is for your greater good and for the good of others who, like you, are pursuing enlightenment. We believe you're test worthy, so here comes our explanation: There is nothing 'out there' that wants to test us. There is no sadomasochistic being in the sky whose chief galactic occupation is to test us, examine us, or cause trials and tribulations to befall us.

THIS WAS SENT TO TEST ME

69

Truth Triage

We are tested by the consequences of our own thoughts, words, and actions. God (Oneness, Divine Consciousness, Divine Mind) is not a testing agency. It does not create negative, harmful, or challenging events just to test our mettle. We do not need cosmic true-false tests or inter-galactic fill-in-the-blank exams to ripen our Earth experience. We may find ourselves facing trials and tribulations, but they come from human missteps – not cosmic examiners.

REPLACEMENT PHRASE

• •

I'm Testing
Myself

THIS WAS SENT TO TEST ME

What This Phrase Assumes

This oft used cliché is most frequently used when destructive acts of nature occur like: hurricanes, earthquakes, floods, tsunamis, tornados, and the like. We'll bet you can't recall when this phrase was used to describe a time when something wonderful happened. (This is not a test. We covered that a few pages ago).

It is really amazing how a cliché like this and its sister phrase, "It's in God's hands," can be attributed to a vengeful Deity. The implication is that Mother Nature is having a bad hair day and has God's permission to do a number on us. This is victim consciousness at its unfortunate finest. It's like putting the fox in charge of the chicken coop. This whole notion springs from embedded theology, theology from our childhood, which places a micromanaging Deity "up there" using natural forces to remind us who's in charge.

GET OVER IT!

● ●

We'd like to share another, more sane, view that does not retail the belief that God made and controls the physical universe. God is Spirit, not matter. God doesn't form physical things. Our bodies, the Earth, and the universe are matter. They are physical things. Spirit is simply Spirit. We're going to get really heavy, so you may want to fasten your seatbelt. It is from our (humankind's) sense of separation from Spirit that we assume form and matter (the entire physical universe) and come into existence. Planets are energetic systems that release energy through thunderstorms, hurricanes, earthquakes, floods, and the like. Water falling on the Earth's surface is part of that natural cycle.

More water or less water is only good or bad from the context of our human consciousness. Water just does what water does. The same thing applies to wind, lava and subterranean pressurized gases. The problem isn't Mother Nature's temper tantrums. The problem is a disrespectful human race who builds towns in flood plains, deforests millions of acres of woodland, and pollutes waterways.

IT WAS AN ACT OF GOD

Truth Triage

The effects of the energetic systems and cycles of the planet are not acts of God. Please take that last statement to heart. They are effects of human consciousness. We are responsible for these "acts" from both a collective consciousness level and a personal consciousness level. Human error consciousness is responsible for building structures in tenuous locations, and for failing to provide adequate safe guards and warning systems to compensate for poor judgment. Floods of various severities come in cycles, and yet we build structures in flood plains. Condos and homes are built on sea shores, in the path of hurricanes, or near earthquake fault lines. These are results of human antics, not "acts of God." We can partner with the planet or continue our adversarial relationship with the planet. The effects of monumental weather events are in our hands.

GET OVER THESE, TOO!

REPLACEMENT
PHRASE

● ●

It Was an Act of
Collective Error
Consciousness

IT WAS AN ACT OF GOD

77

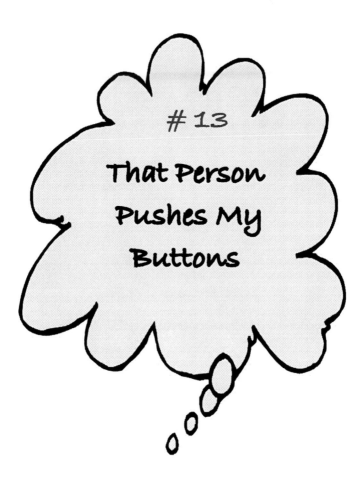

What This Phrase Assumes

This is a metaphor people use when they believe their emotional reaction was caused by someone else. The 'buttons' being pushed are the "not so nice" buttons! Mothers, fathers, brothers, sisters, friends, co-workers, and even strangers – according to this metaphor—push our buttons. These buttons seem hot wired to the most vulnerable sore spots in our personalities.

GET OVER IT!

No one pushes our buttons. In fact, we do not have invisible hot spots that people can activate or push. This phrase is used by people who willingly abdicate their personal power by giving it to someone else. We might just as well say that someone is pulling our strings, or jerking us around, or pushing us around like a spineless mannequin.

THAT PERSON PUSHES MY BUTTONS

81

Truth Triage

The only truth in this phrase is that we react emotionally to what other people are doing or saying. And, we tend to blame others for *causing* these reactions. This phrase is simply another example of our adopting a victim consciousness. Did we say adopting? It's more like we do this so much that we have stayed and built a condominium! It represents our refusal to take responsibility for our own behavior. If 'buttons' are pushed at all, *we're* the ones pushing our own buttons.

Each of us may have sore spots, sensitive areas, points of vulnerability. These are based on our accepted beliefs and attitudes. Our reactions come from these beliefs and are not directly caused by an outer stimuli or catalyst. We choose how we respond or react to another person's words or actions. Someone's behavior is just information. We choose what to do with that *INformation*. The *OUTformation* (our thoughts, words, and actions) is determined by the nature of our consciousness. After all, it's all BS—belief system!

REPLACEMENT PHRASE

• •

I Push My
Own Buttons

THAT PERSON PUSHES MY BUTTONS

What This Phrase Assumes

This seemingly innocent phrase is generally used in two types of situations:

1. *When there seems to be no apparent reason for an event or situation, or*

2. *When something bad happens that has no reasonable explanation.*

When we say, "Everything happens for a reason," we are implying there is an unknown reason that is determined by an external God—the Universe—and our job is to try to figure out where that 'God in the sky' is leading us.

GET OVER IT!

●●●●●●●●●●●●●●●●●●●●●●●

Duh! Of course, everything happens for a reason. But that's not the real reasoning behind this obnoxious phrase. It assigns the locus of control outside of us. There is no anthropomorphic Being in the sky dictating what happens to us or engineering events to teach us lessons or give us wake up calls.

Please say that last sentence aloud before you continue reading. Now read it one more time. We don't mean to belabor this, but put your right palm over your right ear as you read aloud that statement again. The reason we have you do this is so those words don't go in one ear and out the other! (We can hear your groans from here). We want you to 'get' that the presence of God is within you. God-consciousness is in your consciousness and your consciousness is in God-consciousness. God expresses Godness in, through, from you and It is the Real You.

GET OVER THESE, TOO!

EVERYTHING HAPPENS FOR A REASON

Truth Triage

Yes, things happen for a reason. The reason is usually that we decide to do something to project consciousness into outer experience. Sometimes we reason that it is in our best interest to do something, regardless of whether the reasoning is sound or not. Or, what happens could be an "act of nature" (notice we didn't say an act of God) which is the result of an orderly planetary reaction to an environmental stimulus.

So, when we are dealing with a situation or event, we may not know the reason it happened or who caused it. But, we get to choose what reason we assign to the situation. We can bring ordinary human reason, based on material attachments and what our senses are informing us, or Christ Reasoning, based on our Christ-Nature, to bear on the situation.

REPLACEMENT
PHRASE

● ●

I Bring My
Christ Reason
To Everything

EVERYTHING HAPPENS FOR A REASON

What This Phrase Assumes

*We can hear you asking, "What on earth could be wrong with this phrase?" Here goes: This phase is used when we pray **to** God or affirm the kind of prosperity we want. It is about wanting something and then expressing non-attachment to what is wanted because God might have something better in store for us. God might have something better "up His sleeve" and we wouldn't want to interfere.*

GET OVER IT!

● ●

*Don't suffer from a **pain in the ask!** The advice Jesus gave was to ask, believing, and we shall receive. Besides, we do not believe in asking God for anything. We believe that when we pray we claim what is already ours and True in consciousness.*

GET OVER THESE, TOO!

THIS OR SOMETHING BETTER

Truth Triage

In John 11:43 we can read where Jesus raised Lazarus from the dead: "Lazarus, come forth!" Notice he did not walk up to Lazarus's tomb and say, "Yo, Lazarus, come out ... this or something better will happen today." Nor did Jesus say, "Thy will be done."

This phrase is somewhat tied to the concept of "Thy will be done" and, as usual, there is some truth in it. However, when we say, "thy will be done" or "this or something better," we are perpetuating the belief in separation. We are implying that an external deity has a better idea and a specific will for us. We are affirming that a God 'out there' knows better than we do about what we should or should not be, do, or have. To say there is God's will and our will smacks of separation. Our prayers and affirmations must come from the awareness of Oneness, God, Divine Mind, Spirit.

REPLACEMENT PHRASE

This Is
Something
Better

16

Count It
All Joy

What This Phrase Assumes

"Count it all joy" is used is to sugar coat a negative event. Something bad happens and we say, "Count it all joy." While this phrase was used by Myrtle Fillmore to give people hope in dire situations, she really did not mean it in the way people use it today. It appears to say 'give thanks for all things,' but we believe this assumption is what gets us into trouble!

When Myrtle Fillmore questioned why she was not getting well, a message from Spirit said, "You have looked among your faults; now look among your virtues." Realizing she took great pride in the fact that she never let anyone know just how she felt when anything displeased or hurt her, she determined to handle all that came to her, before she 'swallowed it' and allowed it to irritate and weaken her nerves and organs. As she kept her thoughts and feelings truly free, she was restored to strength and normal functioning." (p. 187, How to Let God Help Me)

GET OVER IT!

● ● ● ● ● ● ● ● ● ● ● ● ● ● ● ● ● ● ● ●

Everything in this relative world of form is not literally a joy or good. How many times have you counted on something which never materialized? Unpleasant things happen. Get over it! Disappointments seem to come our way. Get over it! Sometimes we fall out of integrity and choose error thoughts, words, and actions over thoughts based on Divine Ideas that give rise to words and actions. Get over it!

Should we be joyful for unpleasant disappointments? Must we slough off unsatisfying experiences nonchalantly? No! We encourage you not to sugar coat negativity or mindlessly push it down into your subconscious. Keep in mind that in I Thessolonians 5:18, we are told "In everything give thanks" ... not FOR everything! The difference is huge!

COUNT IT ALL JOY

Truth Triage

When properly used, this phrase is similar to "calling it good." The intention was never to imply that a particular event or situation is literally good or full of joy. In *Christian Healing*, Charles Fillmore asserts: "We should not assume that all manifestation is good because the originating idea came from Divine Mind. All ideas have their foundation in Divine Mind, but humankind has put the limitation of negative thoughts upon them, and sees them 'in a mirror, darkly.'"

This phrase is intended to see beyond outer appearances to the Divine (as Divine Ideas) that is always present and "underwriting" everything, yet not literally entering into everything. This is much like not being able to literally find the idea for table in your dining room table. Myrtle Fillmore, in her book *How to Let God Help You,* said that an "unpleasant condition is just temporary, and it is dissolved by the Truth that you are and have been thinking." Everything is based on Divine Ideas, and while Divine Ideas are always Good, that does not mean what we do with them is always good. Unpleasant conditions and error consciousness are remedied with Divine Ideas and Truth when each of these concepts is used productively.

REPLACEMENT PHRASE

● ● ● ● ● ● ● ● ● ● ● ● ● ● ● ● ● ● ● ●

*I Choose Joy
In All Things*

What This Phrase Assumes

This well intentioned cliché is generally used when we do not know what to do about a situation. And so we say something like, "I'm going to surrender this to God." It is also used when we are listening to somebody else's story/drama and then feel led to say, "Surrender it to God." Variations of that heartfelt advice are: "Put it in God's hands," and "Let go, let God." These phrases imply there is nothing we can do about our stories, situations, or dramas. And so we justify our abdication of power by giving it to God. God 'out there' will handle it.

GET OVER IT!

● ●

First and foremost, this cliché assumes that there is a God 'out there,' separate from us, to surrender something to. Raising a white flag and hoping God will see it on His next 'pass' through our neighborhood is surrendering to the illusion and the false assumptions it spins. God is not outside of us physically, nor is God outside of our consciousness. God is not the handyman in the sky who fixes everything.

GET OVER THESE, TOO!

SURRENDER IT TO GOD

Truth Triage

We can and should surrender our human egos (egocentric personalities) to the Oneness. From the Oneness, the Christ (the Idea that is made up of Ideas), we can know how to handle everything in our lives.

REPLACEMENT
PHRASE

● ●

Surrender It To
Your God-Mind

What This Phrase Assumes

This is a Bible-based phrase that assumes God has a specific will for each of us. It assumes our will is separate and different from God's Will.

GET OVER IT!

• •

While we can cultivate our own willfulness, there is no such thing as a God 'out there' who imposes Its Will on us. Nor a Universe out there imposing its will upon us! Phrases like this keep us stuck trying to figure out what God's Will is for us. It can keep us mired in the assumption that "I'll be happy when I know what God's Will is for my life."

GET OVER THESE, TOO!

NOT MY WILL BUT GOD'S WILL BE DONE

Truth Triage

Once again, there is no God "out there" with a micro-managing penchant who has a pre-determined will for us. Therefore, God is not keeping it from us like some big secret! There really is no such thing as God's Will, as it is traditionally understood, that is somehow separate from our will.

Eric Butterworth has this to say about God's Will: "Some persons puzzle over the question, 'How can one distinguish between divine guidance and human will?' The very question implies a duality—a sense of God 'out there' who would or could desire for you something contrary to your personal desires. Divine guidance is not an exterior force acting upon you. It is the seed of your Divinity (the Christ of you) seeking to fulfill its pattern in the out forming process of your life. God could never want for you that which you do not inherently want for yourself." (*In the Flow of Life*, pgs 70, 71)

Butterworth is inviting us to realize that we have the wherewithal to make choices from the awareness that we are one in consciousness in God (Divine Mind). We want to make choices from the Christ (the Idea that is made up of Ideas) and not solely from our ego/ personality.

There's one more thing we want to clear up about choices. We hear people say things like, "I didn't have a choice" or "That person had no choice." Statements like these abdicate our power and resonsibility to manage our lives. They, quite frankly, are cop outs which spring from a victim consciousness. We will manage our lives when we mange ourselves, and we will manage ourselves when we manage our choices.

Oh, and one more thing. We are not the products of our past or the environment in which we find ourselves. What happens to us is the product of our choices!

Unity's co-founder Charles Fillmore has this to say: "The idea of giving up the will to God's will should not include the thought of weakening it, or causing it to become in any way less; it properly means that the will is being instructed how to act for the best. Do not act until you know how to act. 'Look before you leap.'

"This does not imply that one should be inactive and indefinite, waiting for understanding, as do many persons who are afraid to act because they may possibly do the wrong thing; it means that understanding will be quickened and the will strengthened by the confidence that comes as a result of knowledge."

(*Christian Healing*, Pg. 110)

REPLACEMENT
PHRASE

● ●

Not My Willfulness
But My
God-Mind Will
Be Done

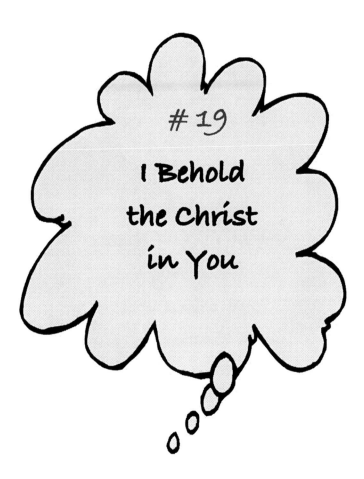

What This Phrase Assumes

When people hear this phrase, it implies that Christ is within the body. It is 'wiener in the bun' theology. This view assumes that the wiener is never the bun and the bun is never the wiener.

GET OVER IT!

● ●

Christ is not the 'wiener' in our somatic 'bun.' Christ is not within our bodies.

GET OVER THESE, TOO!

I BEHOLD THE CHRIST IN YOU

119

Truth Triage

Take a deep breath. Here's the scoop! If Christ is in anything, It is in consciousness. Our consciousness is in Christ Consciousness like sugar dispersed in water, instead of a wiener in a bun. There is an indivisible dynamic at work. When we look at the geography of consciousness, neither 'consciousness' is within the other. Consciousness simply is.

In *Keep a True Lent*, Unity's co-founder Charles Fillmore refers to this universal consciousness:

"WE HAVE NO independent mind; there is only universal Mind, but we have consciousness in that mind and we have … control over our own thoughts, and our thoughts make up our consciousness. By analyzing ourselves we find that we unconsciously separate ourselves into different personalities. We should do this work consciously. We should enter into the understanding that the I AM power is given to us in consciousness, and then join or unify that consciousness with the great Christ Mind." (Pg. 177)

REPLACEMENT
PHRASE

I Behold
the Christ

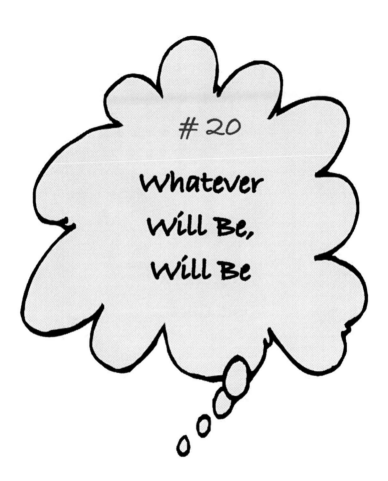

What This Phrase Assumes

Are you humming Que Sera, Sera yet? It's a catcy tune, but we have to say beware! This catchy little phrase quite simply preaches predetermination. Whatever will be, will be—and there is nothing we can do about it. It mindlessly disregards the power of choice.

GET OVER IT!

● ●

We do not live in a universe where everything or anything is pre-determined. We really do have to get over the "crystal ball" notion of an anthropomorphic God 'out there' who predetermines, masterminds, and micromanages our lives.

WHATEVER WILL BE, WILL BE

Truth Triage

Grow out of your fixation with predetermination. God (the Eternal Oneness) is not an anthropomorphic Being in the sky who predetermines, masterminds, or micromanages our lives. We must declare our power and realize that we are the ones who divinely order our human experiences.

This point is well made in the following quote from Charles Fillmore's book, *Christian Healing:* "The absolute freedom of the individual must be maintained at all hazards. God is the one principle; we are all as free to use God as we are free to use the principles of mathematics or of music. The principle never interferes, but if it is to be rightly applied we must develop understanding." (Pg. 112)

Eric Butterworth agrees: "The only pre-destiny in life is the ultimate unfoldment of the divine creature you are. But the direction you take in realizing this out forming of the Christ indwelling will always be determined by your consciousness." (*In the Flow of Life*, Pg. 77)

We'd like to add that whatever will be is up to us, each consecutive moment of now. Whatever will be is the result of the collective action of present moments strung together in the process we call time.

REPLACEMENT
PHRASE

· ·

Whatever Will Be

Is Up To Me

WHATEVER WILL BE, WILL BE

127

What This Phrase Assumes

This is based on the idea that God provides everything ... that God, the Big Guy in the sky, not only micromanages everything, but also provides for everyone. People who use this unenlightened phrase generally use Luke 12:24 to justify their belief in a God in heaven providing everything. Luke 12:24 says:

"Consider the ravens: they neither sow nor reap, they have neither storehouse nor barn, and yet God feeds them. Of how much more value are you than the birds!"

GET OVER IT!

● ●

There is not a God, 'the Big Guy' in the sky or a far off heaven, who provides everything we need in the way most people assume when they hear or speak this phrase.

GOD WILL PROVIDE

Truth Triage

While God is the ultimate Source and Provision for everything, God does not provide goodies like the goodies we provide for the kids on Halloween, Easter, birthdays, and the like. The Oneness (God) is the One Principle, the Divine Process we use to provide for ourselves. God (Oneness) is the Source of the Divine Ideas, Principles, and Processes we use in the relative realm (physical world) to provide for ourselves.

REPLACEMENT
PHRASE

● ●

I Provide
From My
God Nature

GOD WILL PROVIDE

What This Phrase Assumes

This phrase is used when we interpret an event or something someone says or does as a sign from God that gives us permission to take some kind of action—or settle for 'God-ordained' inaction. It is often used to justify a decision we have already made under the guise we have obtained God's approval.

Get Over It!

· ·

We know we have said this umpteen times before, but you are worth the reminder! There is no God 'out there' sending signs and signals pointing us in a certain direction. Think about it, if God does that, then why wouldn't this puppeteer God simply tell us what to do every minute!

When we look for signs or believe we get signs from a God in the sky, what is really happening is that WE are assigning meaning and significance to events and occurrences.

THIS MUST BE A SIGN FROM GOD

137

Truth Triage

Since there is not a God 'out there' orchestrating the decisions and choices we make, God doesn't give us signs. If there's any kind of sign out there, it's the cosmic signature of the Oneness (God) in the form of the omnipresent availability of Divine Ideas and Substance. We live, move, and have our beingness from a constant flow of Christ Consciousness, providing an inner knowing which sustains and guides us according to our conscious awareness.

When our decisions go well ... or not ... we are the ones who interpret the events as signs from God.

REPLACEMENT
PHRASE

· ·

This Must Be
An Inner Signal

THIS MUST BE a SIGN FROM GOD

What This Phrase Assumes

This phrase is used to explain that whatever happens must be good because God is Good all the time, even when from our human awareness it seems bad.

GET OVER IT!

• •

Of course God (Oneness) is Good all the time – in the Absolute Realm (the realm of Pure Spirit). In the relative realm of sense consciousness (the physical world), God is the underlying omnipresence of Good but what we think, say, and do may displace (cover-up, dim, delay) that Goodness.

The Good is readily available in the form of Divine Ideas and unlimited Substance. Substance is like "Spiritual Play-doh." Just like we choose how we shape and form Play-doh, we give shape and form to Substance as we use our imaginations. Substance is formed into beliefs, thoughts, and images. We, individually and collectively, choose how we use that Substance.

GOD IS GOOD ALL THE TIME

143

Truth Triage

God (Oneness, One Mind) is the very essence of Goodness. God (Oneness) underwrites all Divine Ideas, Laws, Principles, and Processes. However, the way we use these Divine Ideas, Laws, Principles, and Processes in the relative realm (the world of sense consciousness) determines if they are used selfishly or altruistically.

Let's use electricity as a metaphor to explain the omnipresence of Goodness. No doubt you are familiar with the generally accepted laws and principles of electricity. We might call these laws *good* in an "absolute sense," when they are not being used but are available for use. However, we can use these laws and principles any way we want. We can use them to warm and light our homes or, 'Heaven' forbid, use them to burn homes to the ground, or injure – or even kill – someone. While the principles and laws of electricity are *good all the time,* how we use them depends on how often we allow our goodness and Godness to shine.

REPLACEMENT PHRASE

• •

God-Mind is

Absolute Goodness

All the Time

24

I'll Get There
When I'm Ready

What This Phrase Assumes

This phrase assumes that we will learn something or achieve something when we are ready. There is a subtle undertone that God 'out there' is the one orchestrating our readiness.

GET OVER IT!

• •

You know what we're going to say! (Hee, hee!)

If it wasn't central to your spiritual growth and human happiness, we wouldn't bother to be so redundant. There is no God in the sky (or "Universe") who readies us by sending us through some sort of predetermined experiential gauntlet which prepares us for some specified human achievement. You may want to read that again – it's a bit wordy. You may go to the next section when you're ready. (We're messing with you).

I'LL GET THERE WHEN I'M READY

Truth Triage

The questions to ask ourselves are:
- What do we want to do? *and*
- Where do we want to go?

If there is something we want to learn or a goal we want to achieve, a certain amount of preparation and readiness is necessary. (Duh-Ha!) Our teaching point is this: we are not apprenticed by a God 'out there' who determines when we are ready. Since we are the point of power in our own lives, we determine when we are ready.

REPLACEMENT
PHRASE

● ● ● ● ● ● ● ● ● ● ● ● ● ● ● ● ● ● ●

I'll Get There
When I Ready
Myself

I'LL GET THERE WHEN I'M READY

What This Phrase Assumes

This expression is used when things come together just right. It assumes that God 'out there' is doing His/Her/Its (you pick the descriptor) thing to make everything work together.

GET OVER IT!

● ●

There is no such workaholic God! God (the Eternal Oneness and Divine Mind) does not unilaterally work things out or micromanage human existence. God (the Eternal Isness) is not in the business of engineering a universe which forces us to abdicate our responsibilities.

IT'S A GOD THING

Truth Triage

God is not an Entity who is in the business of meticulously working out the details of each of our lives. We are the ones who employ our God-Mind (Oneness, the Underlying Spiritual Essence, Divine Mind) to work things out. When everything comes together in some seemingly miraculous way, it is the result of our One Mindedness and heightened Christ Consciousness. It is the outcome of our individual consciousness that has its existence in collective consciousness, which has its existence in the Divine Mind (Divine Consciousness, the Eternal Isness).

Eric Butterworth reminds us: "The light you seek is not somewhere else, but where you are. Don't ask God to guide you or beg God to make the choice for you. Instead, affirm that you are in the flow of light, and God is the light. You are in it. It is in you. It is the reality of you. It is not something to reach for but a Truth to accept. **Know that there is that in you that knows the right and perfect direction for your life and affirm that you are now acting under that guiding light.*"** (*In the Flow of Life*, pg. 75)

*Bold emphasis added by authors

REPLACEMENT
PHRASE

● ●

It's a Consciousness
Thing

Summary Chart

Get Over It	Instead, say:
#1. Let go, let God.	Leash my ego, unleash Godness.
#2. Nothing good ever lasts.	Absolute Good ever lasts.
#3. It just wasn't meant to be.	I'll get it if I mean it.
#4. God has a sense of humor.	I sense the humor in this.
#5. This is a wake up call.	This is a wake myself up call.
#6. It's in God's hands.	It's in my 'God hands.'
#7. This is what I was called to do.	This is what I'm calling myself to do.
#8. The Universe rushes in to fill the void.	I fill the potential.
#9. What goes around comes around.	What we send out is already in.
#10. When the student is ready, the teacher will appear.	When the student is ready, the teacher is apparent.
#11. This was sent to test me.	I'm testing myself.

GET OVER IT!	INSTEAD, SAY:
#12. It was an act of God.	It was an act of collective error consciousness.
#13. That person pushes my buttons.	I push my own buttons.
#14. Everything happens for a reason.	I bring my Christ Reason to everything.
#15. This or something better.	This is something better.
#16. Count it all joy.	I choose joy in all things.
#17. Surrender it to God.	Surrender it to your God-Mind.
#18. Not my will but God's will be done .	Not my willfulness but my God-Mind Will be done.
#19. I behold the Christ in you.	I behold the Christ.
#20. Whatever will be will be.	Whatever will be is up to me.
#21. God will provide.	I provide from my God Nature.
#22. This must be a sign from God.	This must be an inner signal.

GET OVER THESE, TOO!

GET OVER IT!	INSTEAD, SAY:
#23. God is good all the time.	God-Mind is Absolute Goodness all the time.
#24. I'll get there when I'm ready.	I'll get there when I ready myself.
#25. It's a God thing.	It's a consciousness thing.

Who Are These Authors?

Rev. Dr. Paul Hasselbeck currently serves as the Dean, Spiritual Education and Enrichment, at Unity Village, MO. He helped found the only English-speaking Unity Church in Puerto Rico. Dr. Hasselbeck is the author of *Point of Power: Practical Metaphysics to Help You Transform Your Life and Realize Your Magnificence* (which is published in English and Spanish) and has also edited and amplified *Metaphysics I* and *Metaphysics II,* the textbooks used to teach Metaphysics at Unity Village. In his free time, Paul enjoys working out, surfing eBay, collecting vintage art pottery, and enjoying a huge flock of exotic birds. He lives in Kansas City with his partner, Martin.

Listen to Paul's Metaphysical Romp show on unity.fm.

Rev. Dr. Bil Holton, currently shares spiritual leadership responsibilities with his wife, Cher, in the growing Unity Spiritual Life Center in Durham, NC. As a student of metaphysics for over 30 years, Dr. Holton is the author of many books, including *Metaphysical Versions* of all four Gospels. On a personal note, Bil enjoys ballroom dancing, golfing, and taking "Indiana Jones vacations" such as white water rafting, sky diving, and fire-walking. Bil and Cher live in Durham, NC, and have two sons, loving daughters-in-law, and three incredible grandchildren!

You can learn more about Bil by visiting his website: www.metaphysicalbible.net.

GET OVER THESE, TOO!

GET OVER THESE, TOO!